Encyclopedia of Entertainment Finance
(Quick Reference)

Craig R. Everett, PhD

FISCAL PRESS

Notices

This work attempts to identify and define commonly used terms in motion picture deals. These terms are constantly changing and being added upon, and definitions of these terms may not be consistent across the industry. Thus, the reader must use this work at their own risk. The author and publisher are not responsible for any financial damages due to misunderstandings about deal terms discussed in this work.

Product names and corporate names mentioned in this work may be trademarks and are used only for identification and explanation without intent to infringe.

Publisher's Cataloging-in-Publication Data
Everett, Craig R.
  Encyclopedia of Entertainment Finance (Quick Reference) / by Craig R.
    Everett. – p. cm.

ISBN 978-0-988-23742-1 (pbk.)
1.   Motion picture industry—Finance. 2.   Motion picture industry—
    Production and direction. 3. Motion picture industry—Law and
    legislation. I. Title.

ISBN: 978-0-988-23742-1 (paperback)
ISBN: 978-0-9882374-3-8 (e-book)

Fiscal Press
2629 Townsgate Road Suite 235
Westlake Village, CA 91361

CONTENTS

FORWARD AND ACKNOWLEDGEMENTS

Producers and financial professionals in the motion picture industry, without even realizing it, speak in a jargon that is often unintelligible by insiders and outsiders alike. The *Encyclopedia of Entertainment Finance (Quick Reference)* is intended to help people wade through the confusion and blank stares that is fostered by this industry jargon.

I wrote this material primary as a resource for my students, both my MBA students at Pepperdine as well as my executive students in our Certificate in Film & Television Finance program. It became apparent that this guide would be useful to a much broader audience. It is also intended as a study help in preparing for the Certified Media Finance Professional™ (CMFP) exam.

This work is a "quick reference" that is essentially a condensed version of the longer and larger *Encyclopedia of Entertainment Finance* (a.k.a. "EEF"). The difference is that the EEF, in addition to definitions, also contains explanations and examples. At the time of the publication of the quick reference (QR), the full EEF is still an unpublished work-in-progress.

My process for producing the entries that appear in this reference is fairly straightforward. Each time I am exposed to a term that I don't understand, or that I think my students don't know, I jot it down. I then research the term and then try to craft a brief definition that can be understood by both industry insiders and outsiders. The definitions come from my own head onto a blank sheet of paper, so if any of my definitions are materially similar to any definition in another work, it is coincidence. I ask readers to please notify me of any such cases.

The sources of the terms and phrases themselves are three-fold. The primary sources are the remarks of industry guest speakers in my classroom. When they mention a term or phrase with which my students are not familiar, I make a note. As such, I would like to acknowledge the following guest speakers for their remarks that ultimately resulted in additions to my vocabulary list: Philip Alberstat, Bianca Goodloe, Peter Graham, Joseph Chianese, Robb Klein, Larry Mortorff, David Tenzer, Virginia Longmuir, John Burke, Colin Brown, and Jim Irvin.

My second source of unfamiliar terms are various books on film finance that I read on a regular basis. My three favorites are: *The Insider's Guide to Film Finance* (by Philip Alberstat), *The Biz: the basic business, legal and financial aspects of the film industry* (by Schuyler Moore) and *Filmmakers and Financing: Business Plans for Independents* (by Louise Levison). All three of these books are wonderful resources that I highly recommend.

Finally, the third source of unfamiliar terms for my list is the entertainment press, namely *Variety* and *The Hollywood Reporter*. As I read the articles in the trades, I make note of terms and phrases that might be useful to my students.

The industry is constantly changing, so this is a work-in-progress. New show business words, phrases and acronyms appear every year, which means that this guide will never be truly finished. If you notice any errors or deficiencies, please let me know.

- Craig R. Everett, PhD

Part I

Alphabetical Listing
of all Terms

Above the Line

The items that literally are placed above the big bold line that divides the budget top sheet. Refers to the creative elements of a project such as the actors, director, producers and writers.

Access Letter

The document promising future payment that allows the distributor to order copies of the film from the laboratory. See laboratory letter.

Accrual Method

Accounting method where income and expenses are reported when committed rather than when the cash actually changes hands.

Actual Break-Even

The ABE is the point in time where a project shows a profit based on a full distribution fee.

Adjusted Gross

Gross receipts to the distributor minus the costs of cooperative advertising (but distribution expenses are not subtracted).

Adjusted Gross Deal

Agreement between producer and distributor where they split the adjusted gross (the split is often 50/50). The common drawback is the fear that the distributor may skimp on distribution expenses.

Adjusted Gross Receipts

Gross receipts minus off-the-tops.

Advance

Pre-payment for licenses or services rendered. See minimum guarantee, recoupment, or overages.

Advertising Overhead

A flat charge (commonly 10%) on advertising costs that is included in distribution costs for the purpose of calculating the break-even point.

AFTRA

American Federation of Television and Radio Artists. The primary actors guild in the US. Merged with SAG and is now known as SAG-AFTRA.

Ancillary Rights

Rights that may be capable of commercial exploitation that are acquired as a result of the production of a motion picture. Can include television spin-offs, merchandizing rights, prequels/sequels, computer games, books, and music publishing rights.

Angel

A private investor that typically takes equity in the production.

Answer Print

The proof print of a film that combines picture and sound, and is viewed before approving the remaining copies. Also called first trial print.

ASCAP

American Society of Composers, Authors and Publishers. They handle licensing of musical works on behalf of composers/musicians. See also BMI and SESAC.

Assignment by Way of Security

See security agreement. Can also be called security assignment.

At-Source

A contract provision that requires participation or royalties to be calculated based on gross receipts at a defined point in the distribution chain.

Attached

Talent that is contractually (not just verbally) committed to a project.

Back-End

A portion of net profits, after expenses are paid. See monkey points, royalty or participation.

Backstop

An agreement that protects investors against losses beyond a certain limit.

Bankable

Refers to the degree to which an actor is enough of a box-office draw to be able to generate pre-sales if he/she is attached to a project.

Banking Costs

The fees associated with maintaining a bank account for the purpose of collecting receipts.

Basis Point

Defined as one-hundredth of 1 per cent. This is a term used in the context of interest rates (e.g. five basis points is 0.05% and 5% would be 500 basis points).

Below the Line

The items that literally are placed below the big bold line that divides the budget top sheet. Refers to the technical cost elements of the production.

Berne Convention

An international copyright treaty.

BFI

British Film Institute

BMI

Broadcast Music Incorporated. Handles licensing of musical works on behalf of composers/musicians. See also ASCAP and SESAC.

Box-Office Gross

Gross receipts by movie theaters.

Break Costs

The costs (namely lost income) that a bank incurs as the result a borrower paying off a loan early. See also funding breakage costs.

British Actors Equity

A British actors guild, like SAG.

British Film

Any feature film is defined as a British film if it complies with Schedule 1 of the UK Films Act of 1985, as currently amended.

British Tax Shelter

A deal in which the motion picture's copyright is sold to a British company and then in return the production company receives a tax break (this structure was discontinued in 2007).

Budget

The estimated expenses associated with the production of a motion picture. The budget includes four sections: above the line, below the line, post-production, and other. Pre-production costs are not part of the budget.

Cap

The upper limit on the interest rate on a variable rate loan.

Capital Allowances

A tax avoidance scheme in the UK and Canada where 100% of the expenditures related to production and acquisition could written off in the first year rather than depreciated over multiple years.

Cash Break-Even

The CBE is the point when a project shows a profit based on zero distribution fee (or a low distribution fee).

Cash Flow

In the motion picture industry, cash flow means any capital funding for physically producing the project. The correct technical term for this is "cash flow from financing activities." In traditional corporate finance, on the other hand, when people refer to cash flow, they typically are referring either to "cash flow from operating activities" or cash flow from all activities.

Cash Method

Accounting method where income and expenses are reported when cash actually changes hands.

Certification

Refers to an independent accounting firm certifying the cost of production. This is required in the UK to qualify as a British Film.

Chain of Title

The documentation of all the transactions involved in the transfer of the copyright from the author to the producer.

Closing

The execution of all the agreements for all the sources of funding for a motion picture project.

Collateral

Any asset used to secure a loan. For motion pictures, this is commonly the pre-sales agreement.

Collateralize

To secure a loan by pledging an asset of known value.

Collecting Society

An organization (such as BMI, ASCAP or SESAC) that collects licensing fees and royalties on behalf of its members for commercial use of their intellectual property.

Collection Agent

An entity appointed to collect motion picture proceeds and distribute them to the appropriate parties.

Collection Agreement

An agreement between a collection agent and the producer and financiers of a motion picture regarding how proceeds will be collected and distributed.

Completion Bond

A guarantee that principal photography on a motion picture will be completed. Typically the fee for purchasing the completion bond ranges between 2% and 5% of budget.

Completion Guarantee

See completion bond.

Completion Guarantor

A company (often an insurance company) that provides completion bonds.

Contingency

The amount added to the budget to cover unforeseen circumstances. The industry standard is 10% of the budget.

Co-Operative Advertising

Advertising for a motion picture where the cost is shared between the distributor and the exhibitors.

Co-Production

A motion picture project with at least two production companies, generally in different countries, thus allowing access to more tax incentives.

Co-Production Treaty

An agreement between two (or more) countries that allows co-productions to access tax subsidies from both countries.

Copyright Search

A search through the database of the United States Copyright Office to see if a copyright on a story has been previously registered.

Cost of Funds

This can refer to a bank's cost of lending money or, alternatively, to the interest rate charged to a producer by the lender.

Costs Off The Top Deal

A distribution agreement where the distributor and producer take a 50/50 split of gross reciepts minus distribution expenses.

Cross-Collateralization

When a distributor is allowed to recoup losses from one territory with receipts from another territory.

Deal Memo

A term sheet or LOI that lists the relevant details of a negotiation between a member of the cast or crew and the producer. Can be legally binding.

Debenture

This refers to a loan repayable on a certain date. In the motion picture industry it can also refer to the interest charges paid as part of a loan agreement.

Deferee

The party to whom a deferment is paid.

Deferment

A fixed payment, typically promised to creative talent, to be paid out of gross receipts after distribution expenses have been paid and after advances by financiers have been paid back.

Deferred Tax

This is a liability on the balance sheet that typically reflects the amount of tax liability that has been deferred due to tax incentives.

Deficit

Total budgeted cost of the project minus the amount of funding raised. See gap.

Delivery

The physical delivery of the elements of a project.

Derivative Work

A work that is based on a preceding copyrighted work, specifically prequels, sequels, remakes and spin-offs.

Development

The process of preparing a script, attaching talent, and determining pre-sales interest, with the hope that the project will be greenlighted.

DGA

Director's Guild of America. A professional association or guild that represents motion picture directors.

Digital Delivery

Delivery to the exhibitor via satellite, hard drive or other digital media of the electronic version of a motion picture.

Discount

When an agreement (such as a distribution agreement) is assigned to a third party, the face value of that agreement is "discounted" to account for fees and time value of money.

Discounted Cash Flow

The value of a project is calculated using DCF by discounting the each future expected cash flow by the cost of capital and then adding all the discounted cash flows together.

Distribution Agreement

An agreement that grants the right exploit a motion picture via one or more media types in one or more territories for a lump sum payment or a percentage of receipts.

Distribution Expenses Cap

The distribution agreement generally allows deduction of distribution expenses from sales revenue, but only up to a certain limit (or cap).

Distribution Fee

A percentage of gross receipts retained by distributors as payment for their services.

Distributor

An entity that, for a fee or percentage, delivers completed motion pictures to exhibitors, wholesalers and retailers and then collects the associated revenues for the appropriate parties.

Domestic Rights

The rights to distribute a motion picture in the US and Canada (North America excluding Mexico).

Domestic Territory

United States and Canada. Often mistakenly called "US" or "North America."

Droit Morale

The moral right of authors and directors over the artistic integrity of their work. Generally not recognized in the US.

Equity

Generally refers to ownership of a percentage of the production company. Equity holders are paid from net profits, which often don't materialize.

Equity of Redemption

When a property is pledged as collateral for a loan, that pledge is released once the loan is repaid.

Errors and Omissions (E&O) Insurance

Insurance against damages that are the result of honest mistakes or accidently omitted terms in the legal documents. The mistakes must be accidental, not malicious.

Exhibitor

The individual or entity that owns a movie theatre.

Exploit

To utilize a media product in a way that generates gross receipts.

Factor

A financing organization that purchases accounts receivable at a discount.

Factoring

The selling of accounts receivable to a third party (the factor) for an immediate inflow of cash rather than waiting to collect.

Feature Film

A motion picture with a run time of at least 72 minutes.

Film Buyer

An entity that works on behalf of the exhibitors to acquire motion pictures from distributors.

Film Rentals

The portion of gross receipts paid by the exhibitor to the distributor.

Final Cut

The final decision on the editing of a motion picture. By default the producer has final cut unless the director specifically negotiates it in the contract.

Finder

An individual working on a commission basis that finds investors for the project.

First Dollar Gross

A participation defined as a percentage of adjusted gross (gross receipts minus off-the-tops)

First Look

A contract that for a fee grants for a specified period of time the right of pre-emption or first refusal on an intellectual property.

First Trial Print

The proof print of a film that combines picture and sound, and is viewed before approving the remaining copies. Also called answer print.

Floating Charge

A UK concept similar to a floating lien in the US. Allows borrower to secure loan with a pool of potentially changing assets, which can be used, bought and sold while the charge (lien) still floats. If the borrower defaults, then the charge "crystallizes" against specific assets.

Floating Rate

An interest rate that is pegged to a changing index (such as LIBOR) plus a fixed margin.

Foreign Rights

The rights to distribute a motion picture property anywhere other than domestic (US and Canada).

Forward Rate Agreement

An agreement that locks in a fixed interest rate for a loan beginning in the future.

Four-Walling

The practice of the producer renting out a movie theatre (all the seats inside the "four walls") for a given period of time (often one week). The producer then gets 100% of the receipts. This is typically only done when the producer cannot get a traditional distribution agreement.

Free television

Broadcast television received by the viewer via antenna, rather than cable, satellite or internet. See standard television.

Fringes

Benefit costs above and beyond wages (such as social security or pension) for the below-the-line staff.

Funding Breakage Costs

The costs (namely lost income) that a bank incurs as the result a borrower paying off a loan early. See also break costs.

Gap

The difference between the required budget of motion picture and the amount raised from distributors.

Gap Financing

A senior loan, typically from a bank, to cover the gap (difference between amount raised from distibutors and the budget).

Gearing

The debt-to-equity ratio of the production company.

German tax shelter

A sale & leaseback arrangement where the copyright of a motion picture is bought by a German company, triggering an instant tax deduction for the producer. The project is not even required to be produced in Germany.

Grant

Refers to government funding for a project that does not have to be repaid, so it is "free money."

Greenlight

The formal approval of project's financing, allowing the motion picture project to move from development into the pre-production phase.

Gross After An Artificial Break

A deal where the participant gets a percentage of adjusted gross receipts after the rolling actual break even point.

Gross After CBE

A deal where the participant gets a percentage of adjusted gross receipts after the cash break even point.

Gross corridor

A provision in an investment agreement that allows the production company to take a certain percentage of sales off the top in order to keep the company afloat while continuing to market the motion picture.

Gross from a Multiple

A deal where the participant gets a percentage of adjusted gross receipts after a multiple is reached.

Gross participation

An arrangement under which a participant in a motion picture, usually a lead actor, will share in adjusted gross receipts, often first dollar gross.

Gross Receipts

Gross revenues from a motion picture at an agreed-upon point in the distribution chain (generally at-source or revenues received by distributor).

Grossing-up clause

A clause in a loan agreement that requires to borrower to pay extra in order to cover the lender's taxes on the interest income.

Hard Floor

The minimum percentage of net profits guaranteed to the producer regardless of other participations.

Hedge

A side investment (generally options, interest rate swaps or forward rate agreements) to protect against losses from potential changes in interest rates or foreign exchange rates.

Hold-Back

A period of time that a particular window is prohibited. For example, an agreement that no DVDs can be sold until the VOD window closes.

Hollywood Accounting

Inflated overhead charges (production, marketing and distribution) ensuring that the project has a net loss and thus pays no monkey points.

Hollywood Studios

Generally refers to the major studios (or sometimes mini-majors) that are located in the Los Angeles area. They are capable of handling the entire life cycle of a motion picture.

Home Video Royalty

The percentage of home video revenue (typically 20%) that is included in gross receipts for the purpose of calculating participations.

IATSE

International Alliance of Theatrical Stage Employees, Moving Picture Technicians, Artists and Allied Crafts

IFG

International Film Guarantors, a bonding company that closed in 2013.

Increased Costs Clause

A clause in the loan document that requires the borrower to compensate the lender for any additional loans costs resulting from changes in legislation after the loan is originated. See MLA costs.

Independent Film

Any movie not produced by a major motion picture studio. Does not necessarily imply that the motion picture is low budget.

Independent Sales Rep

Handles the international sales of a motion picture for a percentage.

Ink

The act of signing a legally binding agreement, such as a contract.

Intercreditor Agreement

An agreement between all lenders on a deal that delineates who owns what rights and when they get paid.

Internal Rate of Return

IRR is a capital budgeting technique that allows the analyst to determine at what exact rate of return (or cost of capital) the project will exactly break even (NPV equals zero).

Interparty Agreement

An interparty agreement is like an intercreditor agreement, except the intercreditor agreement is just between lenders, and the interparty agreement is between all financiers on the project and spells out who owns which rates and when (or in what order) they get paid.

IRC

Internal Revenue Code. Tax laws are generally referred to by their IRC section in the US.

ITV

Independent Television Commission. Collective name for UK producers and broadcasting companies.

Key Man Clause

This contract clause basically says that if a certain individual is no longer associated with the project, the project is no longer worth doing and the agreement can be terminated.

Kickoff

The start of production or principal photography.

Laboratory Letter

Can refer to either an access letter or a pledge holder agreement.

Lead Bank

The bank that acts as lead manager for the group of banks on a syndicated loan.

Lead Manager

The bank that acts as the lead bank for the group of banks on a syndicated loan.

Letter of Credit

An LC is a letter written by a bank that guarantees that as long as certain conditions are met, payment will be made.

Letter of Intent

An LOI is a letter indicating the intention of the parties to enter into a contract at some point in the near future. It is generally not legally binding, but provides enough assurance and agreement to major terms to allow the contract process to move forward.

LIBID

London Interbank Bid Rate.

Limited Partnership

A partnership that consists of a general partner with unlimited liability and limited partners with limited liability. The limited partners are the investors and the general partner is the manager.

Limited Recourse

A lending situation where the lender has recourse to some borrower assets other then those pledged as collateral.

LIBOR

London Interbank Offered Rate.

Loan Out Agreement

Generally for tax purposes, an individual (like a lead actor) doesn't hire themselves out directly but rather through a production company that they themselves own.

Long-Form Contract

A full contract containing all provisions.

Loss Payee Endorsement

The confirmation from the completion bond provider's reinsurer that they will honor completion bond claims from the producer.

M & E Track

Music & Effects Track. An audio track without any dialogue that can be used for foreign language versions.

Main Titles

The opening credits of a motion picture.

Majors

The major motion picture studios, generally referring to 20th Century Fox, Disney, MGM/UA, Paramount, Sony Pictures, Universal, Warner Bros., Pinewood (UK), and Shepperton (UK)

Margin

For floating rate loans, the interest rate is index plus margin. For example, 1.5% over LIBOR, where 1.5% is the margin.

MCPS

Mechanical-Copyright Protection Society Limited. A UK collection society (like BMI in the US).

Merchandising Rights

The right to sell physical items based on trademarks or copyrighted material from a motion picture.

Mezzanine

Subordinated (junior) debt that usually carries a higher interest rate. Can also include equity warrants (options).

Mini-Majors

Large studios that are not part of the majors.

Minimum Guarantee

The minimum amount the distributor promises to the producer as part of a distribution deal.

Mini-Series

A television series that is essentially a long feature broken up into a number of episodes.

MLA Costs

Additional loans costs resulting from changes in legislation after the loan is originated.

Monkey Points

Percentage points of net profit offered to investors, actors or other participants in the production. A derisive term coined by Eddie Murphy, because this frequently results in no actual payments, due to hollywood accounting that often prevents productions from showing a profit.

Most Favored Nation

A trade status granted to one country by another that promises that no other country will get better import/export terms. Enforced by the World Trade Organization.

MPAA

Motion Picture Association of America. MPAA manages the rating system for motion pictures in the US.

MPEAA

Motion Pictures Exporters Association of America. A trade association that represents the major studios in foreign territories.

Multiple

A factor used as a short-cut in calculating break-even. Distribution costs or negative costs are multiplied times the "multiple" to estimate the break-even point.

Negative Cost

The total cost of the motion picture project up through the production of the finished motion picture, including completion bond and a 10% reserve, but not including P&A or distribution. Literally refers to the total cost of producing the final negative print, from which are created the positive film prints that were used in theatres prior to the advent of digital distribution.

Negative Pick-up

Refers to when a distributor acquires the finished motion picture (for a fixed fee) and then pays the P&A and distribution expenses to get it released.

Negative Pledge

A loan covenant that describes some action the borrower is not allowed to do (for example sell a pledged asset or borrow against it).

Net Asset Value

Book value of the assets of a company minus the book value of liabilities. Equals shareholder equity.

Net Deal

A deal where the participant gets a percentage of net profits.

Net Present Value

NPV is the sum of discounted future free cash flows minus the value invested. It represents the dollar amount of the expected profit of the investment.

Net Profit

Money that is left over after all expenses have been paid. Very few motion picture projects ever show a profit (perhaps by design).

Net Worth

Book value of the assets of a company minus the book value of liabilities. Equals shareholder equity.

Non-Recourse loan

A lending situation where the lender has no recourse to any borrower assets other then those pledged as collateral.

Non-Standard Television

Television other than broadcast (standard television) such as cable, satellite and master antenna systems.

Non-Theatrical Rights

The rights to exhibit a motion picture to a live audience by means of sub-standard projection or by video, where the exhibition of motion pictures is not the primary purpose and when no admission charge is made for the exhibition. Exercise of non-theatrical rights is usually limited to schools, churches, hospitals, prisons, airlines, etc.

Notice of Assignment

A document that is used when the proceeds of a contract (say, a distribution agreement) are used as security for an obligation (like a loan agreement).

NTSC

National Television System Code. The 525-line television code system used in the USA and Japan. PAL and SECAM are used outside the US.

Nut

The agreed-upon operating expenses to be deducted in the contract between an exhibitor and a distributor.

Off-Balance-Sheet Finance

An accounting arrangement to hide a loan or capital expenditure such that it does not appear on the balance sheet. Operating leases and joint ventures are common ways of accomplishing this.

Off-the-Tops

The things deducted from gross receipts to calculate adjusted gross. These items include bank fees, currency exchange fees, collection fees, trade association dues, residuals and taxes.

Optical Sound Negative

The final audio mix is transferred onto a photographic negative film medium so that it can be combined with the visual film negative.

Option

For a defined period of time it is the right to purchase the rights to produce a motion picture. It can also be an option to acquire the services of a specific actor or other talent.

Out of Context Use

When music is used in other scenes or advertisement other than the specific purpose for which it was originally licensed.

Output Deal

The distributor obtains in advance the distribution rights to a number of motion pictures that the producer will make during a defined time period.

Overages

Distribution payments to the producer after the advance or minimum guarantee has been recouped, such as royalties and/or participations.

Overspend

The amount that the actual cost of production exceeds the budget.

P & A

Prints and advertising. The cost of promoting a motion picture and physically getting it into theatres.

P Company

Production Company. The entity formed to produce one or more motion pictures (typically a partnership or LLC).

Packaging

A combination of creative elements such as a script, actor(s) and director which is used to attract interest the interest of investors or distributors.

PACT

Producers Alliance for Cinema and Television. The trade association for producers in the UK.

PAL

Phase Alternative Line. The 625-line code system used in Europe (incluiding the UK) for television. See NTSC and SECAM.

Panning and Scanning

A process by which the aspect ration of a motion picture is converted to legacy television aspect ratio. Since modern televisions and motion pictures now have similar aspect ratios, this process is no longer as important as it used to be.

Pari Passu Pro Rata

Claims are resolved equally and without preference, according the amount of each investor's contribution.

Participation

Generally refers to participation by the talent in the back-end, either a percentage of gross receipts or a percentage of the profit.

Pay or Play

A contract provision which commits the production company to compensate a cast or crew member for a project whether or not that project ever goes into production

PFD Agreement

Production, Finance & Distribution. A comprehensive contract that covers all three of these aspects.

Pick-Up

Refers to when a motion picture made by one studio is then acquired by another. See also negative pick-up.

Pledge Holder Agreement

The laboratory agrees to hold the original film negative until written permission is received from the producers to release it to another party. See access letter and laboratory letter.

Points

Promised share of net profits in a motion picture, measured in percentage points. See monkey points.

Post-ABE Gross

A deal where the participant gets a percentage of adjusted gross receipts after the intial actual break-even point.

Post-Production

The period in a project's creation that takes place after the picture is delivered, or "after the production." This term might also be applied to video/film editing or refer to audio post-production and special effects.

Post-Rolling ABE Gross

A deal where the participant gets a percentage of adjusted gross receipts after the rolling actual break-even point.

Pre-Production

The phase in a media project (typically around 3 months) where the script is finalized and the schedule is produced. Pre-production ends when principle photography begins.

Prequel

A follow-on motion picture that is set in a time perion before the events depicted in another motion picture from which the new story was derived.

Pre-Sale

The sale of rights before a project has been completed (often before production has started). Typically paid as a fixed fee upon delivery, plus overages.

Principal Photography

The actual shooting of a motion picture and the time period during which it takes place (a.k.a. production)

Priority Agreement

The agreement between the financiers about the order in which they get paid. If there is a completion bond, then the guarantor is also part of this agreement.

Private Investor

An individual who is not otherwise connected to the project who invests his/her own money in a motion picture.

Producer's Rep

An agent hired by the producer to handle domestic sales.

Producer's Share of Net Profits

Generally ranges between 40% and 60% of net profit. Net profit is the amount left over after distibution expenses are paid and loans and advances are repaid. It is from the producer's share that monkey points are paid.

Product Placement

An agreement between producers and advertisers to allow a product or logo to be shown in the motion picture.

Production

The phase of the motion picture production that involves principal photography.

Production Accountant

The person that manages finances and dispursements during production.

Production Office

The administrative office for the production company. It is set up during pre-production.

Production Overhead

The expenses associated with management of the production, often taken as a fixed percentage (15% is common) rather than itemized. Not a direct production cost.

Production Price

The amount that the completion guarantor estimates that it will take to complete the motion picture and deliver it. Also known as the strike price.

Production Schedule

The plan of when and how the project's budget will be spent.

Production to Budget Undertaking

The notification given to the completion guarantor by the producer that the project will stay within the budget.

Project

A production is typically referred to as a project while its final existence is still in doubt. The project is no longer called a "project" when pre-production ends.

PRS

Performing Right Society Limited. A UK collection society like MCPS.

Receivables

Refers to accounts receivable. Funds owed to the seller by the buyer after purchasing on credit.

Recoupment

Refers to the distributor's ability to recover (from gross receipts) any advances paid to the producer prior to paying overages.

Recoupment order

The order/priority in which investors or lenders are repaid.

Release Print

A copy of the motion picture actually used by exhibitors. As more and more theatres transition to digital media, this term is becoming archaic.

Remake

A production based substantially on a previously existing motion picture.

Residual

A contingent amount contractually payable under a union or individual agreement to an actor, director or other creative talent associated with the media project.

Revolver

A type of line-of-credit loan arrangement where the producer can immediately access the funds, but the balance periodically must be fully paid back (but then can be redrawn again). Also called a revolving facility.

Revolving Facility

A type of line-of-credit loan arrangement where the producer can immediately access the funds, but the balance periodically must be fully paid back (but then can be redrawn again). Also called a revolver.

Rolling Actual Break-Even

When the ABE point is recalculated from time to time (after the first break-even point) based on cumulative expenses.

Roll-Over Relief

A way to defer capital gains tax liability by reinvesting proceeds from a sale.

Royalty

A percentage of gross receipts (or profits) paid to the original licensor of the work upon which the motion picture is based.

SAG

Screen Actors Guild. Now merged with AFTRA as SAG-AFTRA.

Sale and Leaseback

Often done for tax purposes, this is when the owner of an asset sells that asset to a buyer, then the buyer leases the asset back to the seller.

Sales Agent

An agent hired by the producer to sell the motion picture to distributors. Sales agents typically either receive a flat fee or a percentage of sales plus marketing costs.

SECAM

Sequential Colour and Memory. The 625-line television code system used in France. See PAL and NTSC.

Secondary Rights

Rights that may be capable of commercial exploitation that are acquired as a result of the production of a motion picture. Can include television spin-offs, merchandizing rights, prequels and sequels, computer games, books, and music publishing rights.

Security Agreement

The clause of the loan contract that assigns the motion picture rights to the lender as collateral in the case of default.

Senior Debt

A loan that has top priority for repayment. Can be secured or unsecured.

Sequel

A motion picture based on the same characters and storyline as another motion picture, but that depicts later events.

SESAC

A US organization that handles licensing of musical works on behalf of composers/musicians. See ASCAP and BMI.

Simultaneous Cable Relay

When the over-the-air broadcast is done at the same time as the cable television transmission (for example, a network television broadcast).

Single Purpose Vehicle

An SPV is an entity established specifically for the purpose of owning a particular asset.

Slate

A collection of motion picture projects being financed by a single financier during a pre-determined time period. Slate can also refer to the physical clapboard placed in front of the camera at beginning of a take.

Slate Financing Arrangements

SFA is an arrangement where a motion picture investment entity provides a large amount of funding to a major studio to produce a number of projects. The studio takes a distribution fee and recoups costs, then the net profits are split with the investors.

Sleeper

A motion picture (often low-budget) that becomes very popular despite not being promoted.

Soft Floor

Similar to a hard floor, being the minimum percentage of net profits guaranteed to the producer, but hard floor disregards other participations while soft floor is reduced by other participations.

Soft Money

Funding from sources other than investors, like government sources such as tax incentives, rebates, subsidies, and co-productions.

Source Material

The original intellectual property (such as a book or play) upon which a motion picture screenplay is based.

Spec Script

Refers to a script that was written without a pre-existing contract in place. Thus a writer's first script is nearly always a spec script.

Standard Television

Over-the-airwaves free broadcast television.

Stop Date

Talent will typically have a stop date in their contract, which is the last date that they are contractually obligated to work on the project. This allows the talent to know when they can accept their next opportunity.

Strike Price

The amount that the completion guarantor estimates that it will take to complete the motion picture and deliver it. Also known as the production price.

Studio

Generally refers to one of the major motion picture studios. See majors.

Sub-Distributor

Licensed by the overall distributor to handle distribution and promotion of a motion picture in a specific territory.

Subordinated Debt

A loan with lower legal repayment priority than senior debt. Mezzanine debt is a type of subordinated or junior debt.

Supergap

Gap funding that exceeds 10% of the total budget.

Syndicated Loan

A loan that has multiple lenders, who make the loan as a team (syndicate). One of the lenders typically takes the lead position and handles the administration of the loan for an additional fee.

Syndication

A package of network television episodes from earlier seasons (or for a program that is completely off the air) that is sold to individual television stations or cable channels for broadcast.

Takeover

When a producer breaches the terms of the completion bond, the guarantor can takeover completion of the motion picture.

Talent

This is the industry term for actors, but technically can also include writers and directors.

Tax Credit

Soft money received from a government (state or country) as incentive to attract motion picture production there. Can often be used as collateral for production loans prior to actual receipt of the tax credit.

Tax Haven

A production location (country or jurisdiction) that has very low tax rates. Some common examples are Bermuda, British Virgin Islands, Cayman Islands, Channel Islands, Isle of Man, and Netherlands Antilles.

Tax Incentive

Refers to any tax break offered by a juridiction (state or country) to attract motion picture production.

Tax Shelter

An organizational structure for the production that allows a significant decrease in tax liability.

Tax Transparency

If the investors have equivalent tax consequences whether they are inside or outside of a certain legal structure, then the legal structure is considered to have tax transparency.

Television Rights

Refers to the rights to exhibit the motion picture on broadcast television, cable or satellite.

Theatrical Rights

Refers to the rights to exhibit the motion picture in movie theatres or other public places where admission is charged (or revenue is gained in some other way).

Title

The ownership of the rights to produce a motion picture, established by the documentation of all the transactions involved in the transfer of the copyright from the author to the producer.

Title Search

A contracted search on copyright registrations and trade press for works under the proposed title (or similar titles) of the motion picture to ensure that it is available.

Topline

When the actor's name is placed before the title of the movie in the credits

Trades

Refers to the major industry press outlets, namely Variety and The Hollywood Reporter.

Treatment

A summary (approx. ten pages) of the script that includes just the major scenes.

Treaty Rules

The co-production rules to be followed when two countries have applicable film production treaties.

Triple Track

A type of magnetic audio track for a film.

Turnaround

Refers to the time between when a motion picture project is dropped by one studio and (hopefully) picked up by another studio.

Underspend

The amount that the budget exceeds the actual cost of production.

VFX

Visual effects

VFX breakdown sheet

A list of scenes in the motion picture that contain visual effects and the production items required for each visual effects shot.

VOD

Video on Demand. Generally refers to streaming or downloading of content via the internet at at time chosen by the viewer.

WGA

Writer's Guild of America

Window

The period for which a motion picture is made available for viewing in any particular medium, such as theatrical release, VOD, DVD and television.

Windowing

The act of scheduling the release windows for a particular motion picture (e.g. threatical, VOD, DVD, television)

Working title

The project's name while being made. This is not necessarily the same title under which it will eventually be released.

Part II

Listing of Terms
by Category

Accounting & Finance Terms

Accrual Method

Accounting method where income and expenses are reported when committed rather than when the cash actually changes hands.

Actual Break-Even

The ABE is the point in time where a project shows a profit based on a full distribution fee.

Adjusted Gross

Gross receipts to the distributor minus the costs of cooperative advertising (but distribution expenses are not subtracted).

Adjusted Gross Receipts

Gross receipts minus off-the-tops.

Advance

Pre-payment for licenses or services rendered. See minimum guarantee, recoupment, or overages.

Banking Costs

The fees associated with maintaining a bank account for the purpose of collecting receipts.

Basis Point

Defined as one-hundredth of 1 per cent. This is a term used in the context of interest rates (e.g. five basis points is 0.05% and 5% would be 500 basis points).

Box-Office Gross

Gross receipts by movie theaters.

British Tax Shelter

A deal in which the motion picture's copyright is sold to a British company and then in return the production company receives a tax break (this structure was discontinued in 2007).

Budget

The estimated expenses associated with the production of a motion picture. The budget includes four sections: above the line, below the line, post-production, and other. Pre-production costs are not part of the budget.

Capital Allowances

A tax avoidance scheme in the UK and Canada where 100% of the expenditures related to production and acquisition could written off in the first year rather than depreciated over multiple years.

Cash Break-Even

The CBE is the point when a project shows a profit based on zero distribution fee (or a low distribution fee).

Cash Flow

In the motion picture industry, cash flow means any capital funding for physically producing the project. The correct technical term for this is "cash flow from financing activities." In traditional corporate finance, on the other hand, when people refer to cash flow, they typically are referring either to "cash flow from operating activities" or cash flow from all activities.

Cash Method

Accounting method where income and expenses are reported when cash actually changes hands.

Closing

The execution of all the agreements for all the sources of funding for a motion picture project.

Collateral

Any asset used to secure a loan. For motion pictures, this is commonly the pre-sales agreement.

Cost of Funds

This can refer to a bank's cost of lending money or, alternatively, to the interest rate charged to a producer by the lender.

Deferee

The party to whom a deferment is paid.

Deferment

A fixed payment, typically promised to creative talent, to be paid out of gross receipts after distribution expenses have been paid and after advances by financiers have been paid back.

Deferred Tax

This is a liability on the balance sheet that typically reflects the amount of tax liability that has been deferred due to tax incentives.

Deficit

Total budgeted cost of the project minus the amount of funding raised. See gap.

Discount

When an agreement (such as a distribution agreement) is assigned to a third party, the face value of that agreement is "discounted" to account for fees and time value of money.

Discounted Cash Flow

The value of a project is calculated using DCF by discounting the each future expected cash flow by the cost of capital and then adding all the discounted cash flows together.

Distribution Expenses Cap

The distribution agreement generally allows deduction of distribution expenses from sales revenue, but only up to a certain limit (or cap).

Distribution Fee

A percentage of gross receipts retained by distributors as payment for their services.

Equity

Generally refers to ownership of a percentage of the production company. Equity holders are paid from net profits, which often don't materialize.

Equity of Redemption

When a property is pledged as collateral for a loan, that pledge is released once the loan is repaid.

Factor

A financing organization that purchases accounts receivable at a discount.

Factoring

The selling of accounts receivable to a third party (the factor) for an immediate inflow of cash rather than waiting to collect.

Finder

An individual working on a commission basis that finds investors for the project.

First Dollar Gross

A participation defined as a percentage of adjusted gross (gross receipts minus off-the-tops)

Forward Rate Agreement

An agreement that locks in a fixed interest rate for a loan beginning in the future.

Grant

Refers to government funding for a project that does not have to be repaid, so it is "free money."

Greenlight

The formal approval of project's financing, allowing the motion picture project to move from development into the pre-production phase.

Gross participation

An arrangement under which a participant in a motion picture, usually a lead actor, will share in adjusted gross receipts, often first dollar gross.

Gross Receipts

Gross revenues from a motion picture at an agreed-upon point in the distribution chain (generally at-source or revenues received by distributor).

Grossing-up clause

A clause in a loan agreement that requires to borrower to pay extra in order to cover the lender's taxes on the interest income.

Hard Floor

The minimum percentage of net profits guaranteed to the producer regardless of other participations.

Hedge

A side investment (generally options, interest rate swaps or forward rate agreements) to protect against losses from potential changes in interest rates or foreign exchange rates.

Hollywood Accounting

Inflated overhead charges (production, marketing and distribution) ensuring that the project has a net loss and thus pays no monkey points.

Home Video Royalty

The percentage of home video revenue (typically 20%) that is included in gross receipts for the purpose of calculating participations.

IFG

International Film Guarantors, a bonding company that closed in 2013.

Intercreditor Agreement

An agreement between all lenders on a deal that delineates who owns what rights and when they get paid.

Internal Rate of Return

IRR is a capital budgeting technique that allows the analyst to determine at what exact rate of return (or cost of capital) the project will exactly break even (NPV equals zero).

Interparty Agreement

An interparty agreement is like an intercreditor agreement, except the intercreditor agreement is just between lenders, and the interparty agreement is between all financiers on the project and spells out who owns which rates and when (or in what order) they get paid.

Lead Bank

The bank that acts as lead manager for the group of banks on a syndicated loan.

Lead Manager

The bank that acts as the lead bank for the group of banks on a syndicated loan.

Letter of Credit

An LC is a letter written by a bank that guarantees that as long as certain conditions are met, payment will be made.

LIBID

London Interbank Bid Rate.

LIBOR

London Interbank Offered Rate.

Merchandising Rights

The right to sell physical items based on trademarks or copyrighted material from a motion picture.

Minimum Guarantee

The minimum amount the distributor promises to the producer as part of a distribution deal.

Monkey Points

Percentage points of net profit offered to investors, actors or other participants in the production. A derisive term coined by Eddie Murphy, because this frequently results in no actual payments, due to hollywood accounting that often prevents productions from showing a profit.

Multiple

A factor used as a short-cut in calculating break-even. Distribution costs or negative costs are multiplied times the "multiple" to estimate the break-even point.

Negative Cost

The total cost of the motion picture project up through the production of the finished motion picture, including completion bond and a 10% reserve, but not including P&A or distribution. Literally refers to the total cost of producing the final negative print, from which are created the positive film prints that were used in theatres prior to the advent of digital distribution.

Net Asset Value

Book value of the assets of a company minus the book value of liabilities. Equals shareholder equity.

Net Present Value

NPV is the sum of discounted future free cash flows minus the value invested. It represents the dollar amount of the expected profit of the investment.

Net Profit

Money that is left over after all expenses have been paid. Very few motion picture projects ever show a profit (perhaps by design).

Net Worth

Book value of the assets of a company minus the book value of liabilities. Equals shareholder equity.

Nut

The agreed-upon operating expenses to be deducted in the contract between an exhibitor and a distributor.

Off-Balance-Sheet Finance

An accounting arrangement to hide a loan or capital expenditure such that it does not appear on the balance sheet. Operating leases and joint ventures are common ways of accomplishing this.

Off-the-Tops

The things deducted from gross receipts to calculate adjusted gross. These items include bank fees, currency exchange fees, collection fees, trade association dues, residuals and taxes.

Overages

Distribution payments to the producer after the advance or minimum guarantee has been recouped, such as royalties and/or participations.

Packaging

A combination of creative elements such as a script, actor(s) and director which is used to attract interest the interest of investors or distributors.

Pari Passu Pro Rata

Claims are resolved equally and without preference, according the amount of each investor's contribution.

Participation

Generally refers to participation by the talent in the back-end, either a percentage of gross receipts or a percentage of the profit.

Points

Promised share of net profits in a motion picture, measured in percentage points. See monkey points.

Private Investor

An individual who is not otherwise connected to the project who invests his/her own money in a motion picture.

Production Accountant

The person that manages finances and dispursements during production.

Production Overhead

The expenses associated with management of the production, often taken as a fixed percentage (15% is common) rather than itemized. Not a direct production cost.

Receivables

Refers to accounts receivable. Funds owed to the seller by the buyer after purchasing on credit.

Recoupment

Refers to the distributor's ability to recover (from gross receipts) any advances paid to the producer prior to paying overages.

Recoupment order

The order/priority in which investors or lenders are repaid.

Roll-Over Relief

A way to defer capital gains tax liability by reinvesting proceeds from a sale.

Royalty

A percentage of gross receipts (or profits) paid to the original licensor of the work upon which the motion picture is based.

Sale and Leaseback

Often done for tax purposes, this is when the owner of an asset sells that asset to a buyer, then the buyer leases the asset back to the seller.

Slate Financing Arrangements

SFA is an arrangement where a motion picture investment entity provides a large amount of funding to a major studio to produce a number of projects. The studio takes a distribution fee and recoups costs, then the net profits are split with the investors.

Soft Floor

Similar to a hard floor, being the minimum percentage of net profits guaranteed to the producer, but hard floor disregards other participations while soft floor is reduced by other participations.

Underspend

The amount that the budget exceeds the actual cost of production.

Budget Terms

Above the Line

The items that literally are placed above the big bold line that divides the budget top sheet. Refers to the creative elements of a project such as the actors, director, producers and writers.

Below the Line

The items that literally are placed below the big bold line that divides the budget top sheet. Refers to the technical cost elements of the production.

Budget

The estimated expenses associated with the production of a motion picture. The budget includes four sections: above the line, below the line, post-production, and other. Pre-production costs are not part of the budget.

Contingency

The amount added to the budget to cover unforeseen circumstances. The industry standard is 10% of the budget.

Deficit

Total budgeted cost of the project minus the amount of funding raised. See gap.

Fringes

Benefit costs above and beyond wages (such as social security or pension) for the below-the-line staff.

Gap

The difference between the required budget of motion picture and the amount raised from distributors.

Gap Financing

A senior loan, typically from a bank, to cover the gap (difference between amount raised from distibutors and the budget).

Grant

Refers to government funding for a project that does not have to be repaid, so it is "free money."

Negative Cost

The total cost of the motion picture project up through the production of the finished motion picture, including completion bond and a 10% reserve, but not including P&A or distribution. Literally refers to the total cost of producing the final negative print, from which are created the positive film prints that were used in theatres prior to the advent of digital distribution.

Overspend

The amount that the actual cost of production exceeds the budget.

P & A

Prints and advertising. The cost of promoting a motion picture and physically getting it into theatres.

Producer's Share of Net Profits

Generally ranges between 40% and 60% of net profit. Net profit is the amount left over after distibution expenses are paid and loans and advances are repaid. It is from the producer's share that monkey points are paid.

Production Overhead

The expenses associated with management of the production, often taken as a fixed percentage (15% is common) rather than itemized. Not a direct production cost.

Production to Budget Undertaking

The notification given to the completion guarantor by the producer that the project will stay within the budget.

Soft Money

Funding from sources other than investors, like government sources such as tax incentives, rebates, subsidies, and co-productions.

Tax Credit

Soft money received from a government (state or country) as incentive to attract motion picture production there. Can often be used as collateral for production loans prior to actual receipt of the tax credit.

Tax Incentive

Refers to any tax break offered by a juridiction (state or country) to attract motion picture production.

Underspend

The amount that the budget exceeds the actual cost of production.

Debt Financing Terms

Break Costs

The costs (namely lost income) that a bank incurs as the result a borrower paying off a loan early. See also funding breakage costs.

Cap

The upper limit on the interest rate on a variable rate loan.

Closing

The execution of all the agreements for all the sources of funding for a motion picture project.

Collateral

Any asset used to secure a loan. For motion pictures, this is commonly the pre-sales agreement.

Collateralize

To secure a loan by pledging an asset of known value.

Cost of Funds

This can refer to a bank's cost of lending money or, alternatively, to the interest rate charged to a producer by the lender.

Debenture

This refers to a loan repayable on a certain date. In the motion picture industry it can also refer to the interest charges paid as part of a loan agreement.

Equity of Redemption

When a property is pledged as collateral for a loan, that pledge is released once the loan is repaid.

Floating Charge

A UK concept similar to a floating lien in the US. Allows borrower to secure loan with a pool of potentially changing assets, which can be used, bought and sold while the charge (lien) still floats. If the borrower defaults, then the charge "crystallizes" against specific assets.

Floating Rate

An interest rate that is pegged to a changing index (such as LIBOR) plus a fixed margin.

Forward Rate Agreement

An agreement that locks in a fixed interest rate for a loan beginning in the future.

Funding Breakage Costs

The costs (namely lost income) that a bank incurs as the result a borrower paying off a loan early. See also break costs.

Gap

The difference between the required budget of motion picture and the amount raised from distributors.

Gap Financing

A senior loan, typically from a bank, to cover the gap (difference between amount raised from distibutors and the budget).

Gearing

The debt-to-equity ratio of the production company.

Grossing-up clause

A clause in a loan agreement that requires to borrower to pay extra in order to cover the lender's taxes on the interest income.

Increased Costs Clause

A clause in the loan document that requires the borrower to compensate the lender for any additional loans costs resulting from changes in legislation after the loan is originated. See MLA costs.

Intercreditor Agreement

An agreement between all lenders on a deal that delineates who owns what rights and when they get paid.

Lead Bank

The bank that acts as lead manager for the group of banks on a syndicated loan.

Lead Manager

The bank that acts as the lead bank for the group of banks on a syndicated loan.

LIBID

London Interbank Bid Rate.

Limited Recourse

A lending situation where the lender has recourse to some borrower assets other then those pledged as collateral.

LIBOR

London Interbank Offered Rate.

Margin

For floating rate loans, the interest rate is index plus margin. For example, 1.5% over LIBOR, where 1.5% is the margin.

Mezzanine

Subordinated (junior) debt that usually carries a higher interest rate. Can also include equity warrants (options).

MLA Costs

Additional loans costs resulting from changes in legislation after the loan is originated.

Negative Pledge

A loan covenant that describes some action the borrower is not allowed to do (for example sell a pledged asset or borrow against it).

Non-Recourse loan

A lending situation where the lender has no recourse to any borrower assets other then those pledged as collateral.

Notice of Assignment

A document that is used when the proceeds of a contract (say, a distribution agreement) are used as security for an obligation (like a loan agreement).

Off-Balance-Sheet Finance

An accounting arrangement to hide a loan or capital expenditure such that it does not appear on the balance sheet. Operating leases and joint ventures are common ways of accomplishing this.

Revolver

A type of line-of-credit loan arrangement where the producer can immediately access the funds, but the balance periodically must be fully paid back (but then can be redrawn again). Also called a revolving facility.

Revolving Facility

A type of line-of-credit loan arrangement where the producer can immediately access the funds, but the balance periodically must be fully paid back (but then can be redrawn again). Also called a revolver.

Sale and Leaseback

Often done for tax purposes, this is when the owner of an asset sells that asset to a buyer, then the buyer leases the asset back to the seller.

Senior Debt

A loan that has top priority for repayment. Can be secured or unsecured.

Subordinated Debt

A loan with lower legal repayment priority than senior debt. Mezzanine debt is a type of subordinated or junior debt.

Supergap

Gap funding that exceeds 10% of the total budget.

Syndicated Loan

A loan that has multiple lenders, who make the loan as a team (syndicate). One of the lenders typically takes the lead position and handles the administration of the loan for an additional fee.

Equity Financing Terms

Angel

A private investor that typically takes equity in the production.

Back-End

A portion of net profits, after expenses are paid. See monkey points, royalty or participation.

Backstop

An agreement that protects investors against losses beyond a certain limit.

Equity

Generally refers to ownership of a percentage of the production company. Equity holders are paid from net profits, which often don't materialize.

Finder

An individual working on a commission basis that finds investors for the project.

Gearing

The debt-to-equity ratio of the production company.

Gross corridor

A provision in an investment agreement that allows the production company to take a certain percentage of sales off the top in order to keep the company afloat while continuing to market the motion picture.

Monkey Points

Percentage points of net profit offered to investors, actors or other participants in the production. A derisive term coined by Eddie Murphy, because this frequently results in no actual payments, due to hollywood accounting that often prevents productions from showing a profit.

Net Asset Value

Book value of the assets of a company minus the book value of liabilities. Equals shareholder equity.

Net Worth

Book value of the assets of a company minus the book value of liabilities. Equals shareholder equity.

Points

Promised share of net profits in a motion picture, measured in percentage points. See monkey points.

Private Investor

An individual who is not otherwise connected to the project who invests his/her own money in a motion picture.

Dealmaking Terms

Actual Break-Even

The ABE is the point in time where a project shows a profit based on a full distribution fee.

Adjusted Gross Deal

Agreement between producer and distributor where they split the adjusted gross (the split is often 50/50). The common drawback is the fear that the distributor may skimp on distribution expenses.

Ancillary Rights

Rights that may be capable of commercial exploitation that are acquired as a result of the production of a motion picture. Can include television spin-offs, merchandizing rights, prequels/sequels, computer games, books, and music publishing rights.

Angel

A private investor that typically takes equity in the production.

Assignment by Way of Security

See security agreement. Can also be called security assignment.

Back-End

A portion of net profits, after expenses are paid. See monkey points, royalty or participation.

Backstop

An agreement that protects investors against losses beyond a certain limit.

Contingency

The amount added to the budget to cover unforeseen circumstances. The industry standard is 10% of the budget.

Co-Production

A motion picture project with at least two production companies, generally in different countries, thus allowing access to more tax incentives.

Costs Off The Top Deal

A distribution agreement where the distributor and producer take a 50/50 split of gross reciepts minus distribution expenses.

Cross-Collateralization

When a distributor is allowed to recoup losses from one territory with receipts from another territory.

Deal Memo

A term sheet or LOI that lists the relevant details of a negotiation between a member of the cast or crew and the producer. Can be legally binding.

First Dollar Gross

A participation defined as a percentage of adjusted gross (gross receipts minus off-the-tops)

First Look

A contract that for a fee grants for a specified period of time the right of pre-emption or first refusal on an intellectual property.

Gross After An Artificial Break

A deal where the participant gets a percentage of adjusted gross receipts after the rolling actual break even point.

Gross After CBE

A deal where the participant gets a percentage of adjusted gross receipts after the cash break even point.

Gross corridor

A provision in an investment agreement that allows the production company to take a certain percentage of sales off the top in order to keep the company afloat while continuing to market the motion picture.

Gross from a Multiple

A deal where the participant gets a percentage of adjusted gross receipts after a multiple is reached.

Gross participation

An arrangement under which a participant in a motion picture, usually a lead actor, will share in adjusted gross receipts, often first dollar gross.

Hard Floor

The minimum percentage of net profits guaranteed to the producer regardless of other participations.

Negative Pick-up

Refers to when a distributor acquires the finished motion picture (for a fixed fee) and then pays the P&A and distribution expenses to get it released.

Net Deal

A deal where the participant gets a percentage of net profits.

Output Deal

The distributor obtains in advance the distribution rights to a number of motion pictures that the producer will make during a defined time period.

Pick-Up

Refers to when a motion picture made by one studio is then acquired by another. See also negative pick-up.

Post-ABE Gross

A deal where the participant gets a percentage of adjusted gross receipts after the intial actual break-even point.

Post-Rolling ABE Gross

A deal where the participant gets a percentage of adjusted gross receipts after the rolling actual break-even point.

Priority Agreement

The agreement between the financiers about the order in which they get paid. If there is a completion bond, then the guarantor is also part of this agreement.

Product Placement

An agreement between producers and advertisers to allow a product or logo to be shown in the motion picture.

Recoupment order

The order/priority in which investors or lenders are repaid.

Rolling Actual Break-Even

When the ABE point is recalculated from time to time (after the first break-even point) based on cumulative expenses.

Royalty

A percentage of gross receipts (or profits) paid to the original licensor of the work upon which the motion picture is based.

Security Agreement

The clause of the loan contract that assigns the motion picture rights to the lender as collateral in the case of default.

Single Purpose Vehicle

An SPV is an entity established specifically for the purpose of owning a particular asset.

Slate

A collection of motion picture projects being financed by a single financier during a pre-determined time period. Slate can also refer to the physical clapboard placed in front of the camera at beginning of a take.

Slate Financing Arrangements

SFA is an arrangement where a motion picture investment entity provides a large amount of funding to a major studio to produce a number of projects. The studio takes a distribution fee and recoups costs, then the net profits are split with the investors.

Tax Shelter

An organizational structure for the production that allows a significant decrease in tax liability.

Turnaround

Refers to the time between when a motion picture project is dropped by one studio and (hopefully) picked up by another studio.

Sales & Distribution Terms

Adjusted Gross

Gross receipts to the distributor minus the costs of cooperative advertising (but distribution expenses are not subtracted).

Adjusted Gross Deal

Agreement between producer and distributor where they split the adjusted gross (the split is often 50/50). The common drawback is the fear that the distributor may skimp on distribution expenses.

Adjusted Gross Receipts

Gross receipts minus off-the-tops.

Advertising Overhead

A flat charge (commonly 10%) on advertising costs that is included in distribution costs for the purpose of calculating the break-even point.

At-Source

A contract provision that requires participation or royalties to be calculated based on gross receipts at a defined point in the distribution chain.

Bankable

Refers to the degree to which an actor is enough of a box-office draw to be able to generate pre-sales if he/she is attached to a project.

Banking Costs

The fees associated with maintaining a bank account for the purpose of collecting receipts.

Box-Office Gross

Gross receipts by movie theaters.

British Film

Any feature film is defined as a British film if it complies with Schedule 1 of the UK Films Act of 1985, as currently amended.

Cash Break-Even

The CBE is the point when a project shows a profit based on zero distribution fee (or a low distribution fee).

Collection Agent

An entity appointed to collect motion picture proceeds and distribute them to the appropriate parties.

Collection Agreement

An agreement between a collection agent and the producer and financiers of a motion picture regarding how proceeds will be collected and distributed.

Co-Operative Advertising

Advertising for a motion picture where the cost is shared between the distributor and the exhibitors.

Costs Off The Top Deal

A distribution agreement where the distributor and producer take a 50/50 split of gross reciepts minus distribution expenses.

Cross-Collateralization

When a distributor is allowed to recoup losses from one territory with receipts from another territory.

Digital Delivery

Delivery to the exhibitor via satellite, hard drive or other digital media of the electronic version of a motion picture.

Discount

When an agreement (such as a distribution agreement) is assigned to a third party, the face value of that agreement is "discounted" to account for fees and time value of money.

Distribution Agreement

An agreement that grants the right exploit a motion picture via one or more media types in one or more territories for a lump sum payment or a percentage of receipts.

Distribution Expenses Cap

The distribution agreement generally allows deduction of distribution expenses from sales revenue, but only up to a certain limit (or cap).

Distribution Fee

A percentage of gross receipts retained by distributors as payment for their services.

Distributor

An entity that, for a fee or percentage, delivers completed motion pictures to exhibitors, wholesalers and retailers and then collects the associated revenues for the appropriate parties.

Domestic Rights

The rights to distribute a motion picture in the US and Canada (North America excluding Mexico).

Domestic Territory

United States and Canada. Often mistakenly called "US" or "North America."

Exhibitor

The individual or entity that owns a movie theatre.

Exploit

To utilize a media product in a way that generates gross receipts.

Film Buyer

An entity that works on behalf of the exhibitors to acquire motion pictures from distributors.

Film Rentals

The portion of gross receipts paid by the exhibitor to the distributor.

Foreign Rights

The rights to distribute a motion picture property anywhere other than domestic (US and Canada).

Four-Walling

The practice of the producer renting out a movie theatre (all the seats inside the "four walls") for a given period of time (often one week). The producer then gets 100% of the receipts. This is typically only done when the producer cannot get a traditional distribution agreement.

Gross corridor

A provision in an investment agreement that allows the production company to take a certain percentage of sales off the top in order to keep the company afloat while continuing to market the motion picture.

Gross Receipts

Gross revenues from a motion picture at an agreed-upon point in the distribution chain (generally at-source or revenues received by distributor).

Hold-Back

A period of time that a particular window is prohibited. For example, an agreement that no DVDs can be sold until the VOD window closes.

Home Video Royalty

The percentage of home video revenue (typically 20%) that is included in gross receipts for the purpose of calculating participations.

Independent Sales Rep

Handles the international sales of a motion picture for a percentage.

Letter of Credit

An LC is a letter written by a bank that guarantees that as long as certain conditions are met, payment will be made.

Minimum Guarantee

The minimum amount the distributor promises to the producer as part of a distribution deal.

Negative Pick-up

Refers to when a distributor acquires the finished motion picture (for a fixed fee) and then pays the P&A and distribution expenses to get it released.

Non-Theatrical Rights

The rights to exhibit a motion picture to a live audience by means of sub-standard projection or by video, where the exhibition of motion pictures is not the primary purpose and when no admission charge is made for the exhibition. Exercise of non-theatrical rights is usually limited to schools, churches, hospitals, prisons, airlines, etc.

Nut

The agreed-upon operating expenses to be deducted in the contract between an exhibitor and a distributor.

Off-the-Tops

The things deducted from gross receipts to calculate adjusted gross. These items include bank fees, currency exchange fees, collection fees, trade association dues, residuals and taxes.

Output Deal

The distributor obtains in advance the distribution rights to a number of motion pictures that the producer will make during a defined time period.

Overages

Distribution payments to the producer after the advance or minimum guarantee has been recouped, such as royalties and/or participations.

P & A

Prints and advertising. The cost of promoting a motion picture and physically getting it into theatres.

PFD Agreement

Production, Finance & Distribution. A comprehensive contract that covers all three of these aspects.

Pre-Sale

The sale of rights before a project has been completed (often before production has started). Typically paid as a fixed fee upon delivery, plus overages.

Producer's Rep

An agent hired by the producer to handle domestic sales.

Producer's Share of Net Profits

Generally ranges between 40% and 60% of net profit. Net profit is the amount left over after distibution expenses are paid and loans and advances are repaid. It is from the producer's share that monkey points are paid.

Recoupment

Refers to the distributor's ability to recover (from gross receipts) any advances paid to the producer prior to paying overages.

Sales Agent

An agent hired by the producer to sell the motion picture to distributors. Sales agents typically either receive a flat fee or a percentage of sales plus marketing costs.

Sub-Distributor

Licensed by the overall distributor to handle distribution and promotion of a motion picture in a specific territory.

Television Rights

Refers to the rights to exhibit the motion picture on broadcast television, cable or satellite.

Theatrical Rights

Refers to the rights to exhibit the motion picture in movie theatres or other public places where admission is charged (or revenue is gained in some other way).

Turnaround

Refers to the time between when a motion picture project is dropped by one studio and (hopefully) picked up by another studio.

VOD

Video on Demand. Generally refers to streaming or downloading of content via the internet at at time chosen by the viewer.

Window

The period for which a motion picture is made available for viewing in any particular medium, such as theatrical release, VOD, DVD and television.

Windowing

The act of scheduling the release windows for a particular motion picture (e.g. threatrical, VOD, DVD, television)

Risk Management Terms

Completion Bond

A guarantee that principal photography on a motion picture will be completed. Typically the fee for purchasing the completion bond ranges between 2% and 5% of budget.

Completion Guarantee

See completion bond.

Completion Guarantor

A company (often an insurance company) that provides completion bonds.

Errors and Omissions (E&O) Insurance

Insurance against damages that are the result of honest mistakes or accidently omitted terms in the legal documents. The mistakes must be accidental, not malicious.

Hedge

A side investment (generally options, interest rate swaps or forward rate agreements) to protect against losses from potential changes in interest rates or foreign exchange rates.

IFG

International Film Guarantors, a bonding company that closed in 2013.

Loss Payee Endorsement

The confirmation from the completion bond provider's reinsurer that they will honor completion bond claims from the producer.

Production Price

The amount that the completion guarantor estimates that it will take to complete the motion picture and deliver it. Also known as the strike price.

Production to Budget Undertaking

The notification given to the completion guarantor by the producer that the project will stay within the budget.

Strike Price

The amount that the completion guarantor estimates that it will take to complete the motion picture and deliver it. Also known as the production price.

Takeover

When a producer breaches the terms of the completion bond, the guarantor can takeover completion of the motion picture.

Production Terms

Access Letter

The document promising future payment that allows the distributor to order copies of the film from the laboratory. See laboratory letter.

Certification

Refers to an independent accounting firm certifying the cost of production. This is required in the UK to qualify as a British Film.

Co-Production

A motion picture project with at least two production companies, generally in different countries, thus allowing access to more tax incentives.

Co-Production Treaty

An agreement between two (or more) countries that allows co-productions to access tax subsidies from both countries.

Delivery

The physical delivery of the elements of a project.

Development

The process of preparing a script, attaching talent, and determining pre-sales interest, with the hope that the project will be greenlighted.

Feature Film

A motion picture with a run time of at least 72 minutes.

Final Cut

The final decision on the editing of a motion picture. By default the producer has final cut unless the director specifically negotiates it in the contract.

Greenlight

The formal approval of project's financing, allowing the motion picture project to move from development into the pre-production phase.

Kickoff

The start of production or principal photography.

Main Titles

The opening credits of a motion picture.

Post-Production

The period in a project's creation that takes place after the picture is delivered, or "after the production." This term might also be applied to video/film editing or refer to audio post-production and special effects.

Pre-Production

The phase in a media project (typically around 3 months) where the script is finalized and the schedule is produced. Pre-production ends when principle photography begins.

Prequel

A follow-on motion picture that is set in a time perion before the events depicted in another motion picture from which the new story was derived.

Principal Photography

The actual shooting of a motion picture and the time period during which it takes place (a.k.a. production)

Production

The phase of the motion picture production that involves principal photography.

Production Accountant

The person that manages finances and dispursements during production.

Production Office

The administrative office for the production company. It is set up during pre-production.

Production Schedule

The plan of when and how the project's budget will be spent.

Project

A production is typically referred to as a project while its final existence is still in doubt. The project is no longer called a "project" when pre-production ends.

Release Print

A copy of the motion picture actually used by exhibitors. As more and more theatres transition to digital media, this term is becoming archaic.

Stop Date

Talent will typically have a stop date in their contract, which is the last date that they are contractually obligated to work on the project. This allows the talent to know when they can accept their next opportunity.

Working title

The project's name while being made. This is not necessarily the same title under which it will eventually be released.

Human Resources Terms

Above the Line

The items that literally are placed above the big bold line that divides the budget top sheet. Refers to the creative elements of a project such as the actors, director, producers and writers.

Advance

Pre-payment for licenses or services rendered. See minimum guarantee, recoupment, or overages.

AFTRA

American Federation of Television and Radio Artists. The primary actors guild in the US. Merged with SAG and is now known as SAG-AFTRA.

Attached

Talent that is contractually (not just verbally) committed to a project.

Bankable

Refers to the degree to which an actor is enough of a box-office draw to be able to generate pre-sales if he/she is attached to a project.

Below the Line

The items that literally are placed below the big bold line that divides the budget top sheet. Refers to the technical cost elements of the production.

British Actors Equity

A British actors guild, like SAG.

DGA

Director's Guild of America. A professional association or guild that represents motion picture directors.

Fringes

Benefit costs above and beyond wages (such as social security or pension) for the below-the-line staff.

Gross participation

An arrangement under which a participant in a motion picture, usually a lead actor, will share in adjusted gross receipts, often first dollar gross.

IATSE

International Alliance of Theatrical Stage Employees, Moving Picture Technicians, Artists and Allied Crafts

Key Man Clause

This contract clause basically says that if a certain individual is no longer associated with the project, the project is no longer worth doing and the agreement can be terminated.

Loan Out Agreement

Generally for tax purposes, an individual (like a lead actor) doesn't hire themselves out directly but rather through a production company that they themselves own.

Packaging

A combination of creative elements such as a script, actor(s) and director which is used to attract interest the interest of investors or distributors.

Pay or Play

A contract provision which commits the production company to compensate a cast or crew member for a project whether or not that project ever goes into production

Residual

A contingent amount contractually payable under a union or individual agreement to an actor, director or other creative talent associated with the media project.

SAG

Screen Actors Guild. Now merged with AFTRA as SAG-AFTRA.

Stop Date

Talent will typically have a stop date in their contract, which is the last date that they are contractually obligated to work on the project. This allows the talent to know when they can accept their next opportunity.

Talent

This is the industry term for actors, but technically can also include writers and directors.

Topline

When the actor's name is placed before the title of the movie in the credits

WGA

Writer's Guild of America

Government Terms

British Tax Shelter

A deal in which the motion picture's copyright is sold to a British company and then in return the production company receives a tax break (this structure was discontinued in 2007).

Capital Allowances

A tax avoidance scheme in the UK and Canada where 100% of the expenditures related to production and acquisition could written off in the first year rather than depreciated over multiple years.

Co-Production Treaty

An agreement between two (or more) countries that allows co-productions to access tax subsidies from both countries.

Deferred Tax

This is a liability on the balance sheet that typically reflects the amount of tax liability that has been deferred due to tax incentives.

German tax shelter

A sale & leaseback arrangement where the copyright of a motion picture is bought by a German company, triggering an instant tax deduction for the producer. The project is not even required to be produced in Germany.

Grant

Refers to government funding for a project that does not have to be repaid, so it is "free money."

Increased Costs Clause

A clause in the loan document that requires the borrower to compensate the lender for any additional loans costs resulting from changes in legislation after the loan is originated. See MLA costs.

IRC

Internal Revenue Code. Tax laws are generally referred to by their IRC section in the US.

MLA Costs

Additional loans costs resulting from changes in legislation after the loan is originated.

Most Favored Nation

A trade status granted to one country by another that promises that no other country will get better import/export terms. Enforced by the World Trade Organization.

Roll-Over Relief

A way to defer capital gains tax liability by reinvesting proceeds from a sale.

Soft Money

Funding from sources other than investors, like government sources such as tax incentives, rebates, subsidies, and co-productions.

Tax Credit

Soft money received from a government (state or country) as incentive to attract motion picture production there. Can often be used as collateral for production loans prior to actual receipt of the tax credit.

Tax Haven

A production location (country or jurisdiction) that has very low tax rates. Some common examples are Bermuda, British Virgin Islands, Cayman Islands, Channel Islands, Isle of Man, and Netherlands Antilles.

Tax Incentive

Refers to any tax break offered by a juridiction (state or country) to attract motion picture production.

Tax Shelter

An organizational structure for the production that allows a significant decrease in tax liability.

Tax Transparency

If the investors have equivalent tax consequences whether they are inside or outside of a certain legal structure, then the legal structure is considered to have tax transparency.

Treaty Rules

The co-production rules to be followed when two countries have applicable film production treaties.

Legal Terms

Access Letter

The document promising future payment that allows the distributor to order copies of the film from the laboratory. See laboratory letter.

Ancillary Rights

Rights that may be capable of commercial exploitation that are acquired as a result of the production of a motion picture. Can include television spin-offs, merchandizing rights, prequels/sequels, computer games, books, and music publishing rights.

ASCAP

American Society of Composers, Authors and Publishers. They handle licensing of musical works on behalf of composers/musicians. See also BMI and SESAC.

Assignment by Way of Security

See security agreement. Can also be called security assignment.

At-Source

A contract provision that requires participation or royalties to be calculated based on gross receipts at a defined point in the distribution chain.

Attached

Talent that is contractually (not just verbally) committed to a project.

Berne Convention

An international copyright treaty.

Certification

Refers to an independent accounting firm certifying the cost of production. This is required in the UK to qualify as a British Film.

Chain of Title

The documentation of all the transactions involved in the transfer of the copyright from the author to the producer.

Collecting Society

An organization (such as BMI, ASCAP or SESAC) that collects licensing fees and royalties on behalf of its members for commercial use of their intellectual property.

Copyright Search

A search through the database of the United States Copyright Office to see if a copyright on a story has been previously registered.

Deal Memo

A term sheet or LOI that lists the relevant details of a negotiation between a member of the cast or crew and the producer. Can be legally binding.

Delivery

The physical delivery of the elements of a project.

Derivative Work

A work that is based on a preceding copyrighted work, specifically prequels, sequels, remakes and spin-offs.

Distribution Agreement

An agreement that grants the right exploit a motion picture via one or more media types in one or more territories for a lump sum payment or a percentage of receipts.

Domestic Rights

The rights to distribute a motion picture in the US and Canada (North America excluding Mexico).

Domestic Territory

United States and Canada. Often mistakenly called "US" or "North America."

Droit Morale

The moral right of authors and directors over the artistic integrity of their work. Generally not recognized in the US.

First Look

A contract that for a fee grants for a specified period of time the right of pre-emption or first refusal on an intellectual property.

Foreign Rights

The rights to distribute a motion picture property anywhere other than domestic (US and Canada).

German tax shelter

A sale & leaseback arrangement where the copyright of a motion picture is bought by a German company, triggering an instant tax deduction for the producer. The project is not even required to be produced in Germany.

Ink

The act of signing a legally binding agreement, such as a contract.

Intercreditor Agreement

An agreement between all lenders on a deal that delineates who owns what rights and when they get paid.

Interparty Agreement

An interparty agreement is like an intercreditor agreement, except the intercreditor agreement is just between lenders, and the interparty agreement is between all financiers on the project and spells out who owns which rates and when (or in what order) they get paid.

Key Man Clause

This contract clause basically says that if a certain individual is no longer associated with the project, the project is no longer worth doing and the agreement can be terminated.

Laboratory Letter

Can refer to either an access letter or a pledge holder agreement.

Letter of Intent

An LOI is a letter indicating the intention of the parties to enter into a contract at some point in the near future. It is generally not legally binding, but provides enough assurance and agreement to major terms to allow the contract process to move forward.

Limited Partnership

A partnership that consists of a general partner with unlimited liability and limited partners with limited liability. The limited partners are the investors and the general partner is the manager.

Loan Out Agreement

Generally for tax purposes, an individual (like a lead actor) doesn't hire themselves out directly but rather through a production company that they themselves own.

Long-Form Contract

A full contract containing all provisions.

Merchandising Rights

The right to sell physical items based on trademarks or copyrighted material from a motion picture.

Negative Pledge

A loan covenant that describes some action the borrower is not allowed to do (for example sell a pledged asset or borrow against it).

Non-Recourse loan

A lending situation where the lender has no recourse to any borrower assets other then those pledged as collateral.

Notice of Assignment

A document that is used when the proceeds of a contract (say, a distribution agreement) are used as security for an obligation (like a loan agreement).

Option

For a defined period of time it is the right to purchase the rights to produce a motion picture. It can also be an option to acquire the services of a specific actor or other talent.

Out of Context Use

When music is used in other scenes or advertisement other than the specific purpose for which it was originally licensed.

P Company

Production Company. The entity formed to produce one or more motion pictures (typically a partnership or LLC).

Pari Passu Pro Rata

Claims are resolved equally and without preference, according the amount of each investor's contribution.

PFD Agreement

Production, Finance & Distribution. A comprehensive contract that covers all three of these aspects.

Pledge Holder Agreement

The laboratory agrees to hold the original film negative until written permission is received from the producers to release it to another party. See access letter and laboratory letter.

Production Office

The administrative office for the production company. It is set up during pre-production.

Residual

A contingent amount contractually payable under a union or individual agreement to an actor, director or other creative talent associated with the media project.

Secondary Rights

Rights that may be capable of commercial exploitation that are acquired as a result of the production of a motion picture. Can include television spin-offs, merchandizing rights, prequels and sequels, computer games, books, and music publishing rights.

Security Agreement

The clause of the loan contract that assigns the motion picture rights to the lender as collateral in the case of default.

Single Purpose Vehicle

An SPV is an entity established specifically for the purpose of owning a particular asset.

Source Material

The original intellectual property (such as a book or play) upon which a motion picture screenplay is based.

Takeover

When a producer breaches the terms of the completion bond, the guarantor can takeover completion of the motion picture.

Title

The ownership of the rights to produce a motion picture, established by the documentation of all the transactions involved in the transfer of the copyright from the author to the producer.

Title Search

A contracted search on copyright registrations and trade press for works under the proposed title (or similar titles) of the motion picture to ensure that it is available.

Treatment

A summary (approx. ten pages) of the script that includes just the major scenes.

Treaty Rules

The co-production rules to be followed when two countries have applicable film production treaties.

Entertainment Industry Terms

AFTRA

American Federation of Television and Radio Artists. The primary actors guild in the US. Merged with SAG and is now known as SAG-AFTRA.

ASCAP

American Society of Composers, Authors and Publishers. They handle licensing of musical works on behalf of composers/musicians. See also BMI and SESAC.

BFI

British Film Institute

BMI

Broadcast Music Incorporated. Handles licensing of musical works on behalf of composers/musicians. See also ASCAP and SESAC.

British Actors Equity

A British actors guild, like SAG.

British Film

Any feature film is defined as a British film if it complies with Schedule 1 of the UK Films Act of 1985, as currently amended.

Collecting Society

An organization (such as BMI, ASCAP or SESAC) that collects licensing fees and royalties on behalf of its members for commercial use of their intellectual property.

Development

The process of preparing a script, attaching talent, and determining pre-sales interest, with the hope that the project will be greenlighted.

DGA

Director's Guild of America. A professional association or guild that represents motion picture directors.

Free television

Broadcast television received by the viewer via antenna, rather than cable, satellite or internet. See standard television.

Hollywood Accounting

Inflated overhead charges (production, marketing and distribution) ensuring that the project has a net loss and thus pays no monkey points.

Hollywood Studios

Generally refers to the major studios (or sometimes mini-majors) that are located in the Los Angeles area. They are capable of handling the entire life cycle of a motion picture.

IATSE

International Alliance of Theatrical Stage Employees, Moving Picture Technicians, Artists and Allied Crafts

Independent Film

Any movie not produced by a major motion picture studio. Does not necessarily imply that the motion picture is low budget.

Ink

The act of signing a legally binding agreement, such as a contract.

ITV

Independent Television Commission. Collective name for UK producers and broadcasting companies.

Majors

The major motion picture studios, generally referring to 20th Century Fox, Disney, MGM/UA, Paramount, Sony Pictures, Universal, Warner Bros., Pinewood (UK), and Shepperton (UK)

MCPS

Mechanical-Copyright Protection Society Limited. A UK collection society (like BMI in the US).

Mini-Majors

Large studios that are not part of the majors.

Mini-Series

A television series that is essentially a long feature broken up into a number of episodes.

MPAA

Motion Picture Association of America. MPAA manages the rating system for motion pictures in the US.

MPEAA

Motion Pictures Exporters Association of America. A trade association that represents the major studios in foreign territories.

PACT

Producers Alliance for Cinema and Television. The trade association for producers in the UK.

PRS

Performing Right Society Limited. A UK collection society like MCPS.

Remake

A production based substantially on a previously existing motion picture.

SAG

Screen Actors Guild. Now merged with AFTRA as SAG-AFTRA.

Sequel

A motion picture based on the same characters and storyline as another motion picture, but that depicts later events.

SESAC

A US organization that handles licensing of musical works on behalf of composers/musicians. See ASCAP and BMI.

Sleeper

A motion picture (often low-budget) that becomes very popular despite not being promoted.

Spec Script

Refers to a script that was written without a pre-existing contract in place. Thus a writer's first script is nearly always a spec script.

Studio

Generally refers to one of the major motion picture studios. See majors.

Syndication

A package of network television episodes from earlier seasons (or for a program that is completely off the air) that is sold to individual television stations or cable channels for broadcast.

Talent

This is the industry term for actors, but technically can also include writers and directors.

Trades

Refers to the major industry press outlets, namely Variety and The Hollywood Reporter.

Treatment

A summary (approx. ten pages) of the script that includes just the major scenes.

WGA

Writer's Guild of America

Television Terms

Free television

Broadcast television received by the viewer via antenna, rather than cable, satellite or internet. See standard television.

Mini-Series

A television series that is essentially a long feature broken up into a number of episodes.

Non-Standard Television

Television other than broadcast (standard television) such as cable, satellite and master antenna systems.

NTSC

National Television System Code. The 525-line television code system used in the USA and Japan. PAL and SECAM are used outside the US.

PAL

Phase Alternative Line. The 625-line code system used in Europe (incluized the UK) for television. See NTSC and SECAM.

Panning and Scanning

A process by which the aspect ration of a motion picture is converted to legacy television aspect ratio. Since modern televisions and motion pictures now have similar aspect ratios, this process is no longer as important as it used to be.

SECAM

Sequential Colour and Memory. The 625-line television code system used in France. See PAL and NTSC.

Simultaneous Cable Relay

When the over-the-air broadcast is done at the same time as the cable television transmission (for example, a network television broadcast).

Standard Television

Over-the-airwaves free broadcast television.

Syndication

A package of network television episodes from earlier seasons (or for a program that is completely off the air) that is sold to individual television stations or cable channels for broadcast.

Television Rights

Refers to the rights to exhibit the motion picture on broadcast television, cable or satellite.

Technical Terms

Answer Print

The proof print of a film that combines picture and sound, and is viewed before approving the remaining copies. Also called first trial print.

First Trial Print

The proof print of a film that combines picture and sound, and is viewed before approving the remaining copies. Also called answer print.

Laboratory Letter

Can refer to either an access letter or a pledge holder agreement.

M & E Track

Music & Effects Track. An audio track without any dialogue that can be used for foreign language versions.

NTSC

National Television System Code. The 525-line television code system used in the USA and Japan. PAL and SECAM are used outside the US.

Optical Sound Negative

The final audio mix is transferred onto a photographic negative film medium so that it can be combined with the visual film negative.

PAL

Phase Alternative Line. The 625-line code system used in Europe (includuing the UK) for television. See NTSC and SECAM.

Panning and Scanning

A process by which the aspect ration of a motion picture is converted to legacy television aspect ratio. Since modern televisions and motion pictures now have similar aspect ratios, this process is no longer as important as it used to be.

Release Print

A copy of the motion picture actually used by exhibitors. As more and more theatres transition to digital media, this term is becoming archaic.

SECAM

Sequential Colour and Memory. The 625-line television code system used in France. See PAL and NTSC.

Simultaneous Cable Relay

When the over-the-air broadcast is done at the same time as the cable television transmission (for example, a network television broadcast).

Triple Track

A type of magnetic audio track for a film.

VFX

Visual effects

VFX breakdown sheet

A list of scenes in the motion picture that contain visual effects and the production items required for each visual effects shot.

NOTES

NOTES

NOTES

CPSIA information can be obtained
at www.ICGtesting.com
Printed in the USA
FSHW022053021220
76539FS